Lifelines

Threads of Grace through Seasons of Change

by

Alla Renée Bozarth

SHEED & WARD
Kansas City

To friends seen and unseen
who throw us lifelines
and re-awaken our receptivity
to grace.

Sheed & Ward is a service of the National Catholic Reporter Publishing Company.

Alla Renée Bozarth
ISBN: 1-55612-704-9

Published by: Sheed & Ward
                 115 E. Armour Blvd.
                 P.O. Box 419492
                 Kansas City, MO 64141-6492

To order, call: (800) 333-7373

Illustrations © 1995 by Maureen Noonan
Cover design by James F. Brisson

Contents

Lifelines

Threads of Grace through Seasons of Change

Spinningwoman God

Whole-unto-Herself
but needing us,
She busies Herself
with the universe—

Her cosmos is more
than cosmetic.
She needs to touch,
hold, and listen, so
She gives birth
to a creation
needing to be
touched, held, and heard.

Her body the spindle shank
of spun light, we Her spun gold,
Her opening gyre, Her choreography
of Grace—Spinner God unwinds
Herself into creation, a fiery twirl,
a twirling fire, a circle dance,
She dances the round with us,
forming her favorite shapes
in a rounding motion,
an open embrace.

The double helix,
the essential partnership
of creation, the Great Duet,
the Pas de Deux that generates
Life and honey spun stars.
In love She dances us on,
again and again one into two
and two into one—
more than one I,
more than one You,
She Who Is
        gracious
She Who Is
        friendly
She Who Is
        becoming
Befriends us anew
with each turn of Her spool,
befriending all beings
with the dance of Her hand,
playing music with Her spheres,
and weaving complexities,
infinities, and making braids.

Transition: A Time of Trust and Grace

As I WRITE, IT IS MID-AUTUMN, A SEASON that evokes in me the most extreme feelings. Glancing out my window, I see a blaze of gold, painted across the hills of oak and maple. Driving up my hill into town, I am surrounded by amber canopies of leaves, and overhanging bronze and scarlet archways surpassing cathedral art—awe-inspiring. My eye is fed with beauty everywhere, and my soul is filled. And yet—the long, lavish warmth of summer is gone. Every day, there is less light between nightfalls. As I acknowledge the great beauty of Nature in her season of leaving green in a dying glory, I grieve the loss of summer days. I dread the coming of winter with its long nights and frequently grey days. I resist. Although my water pipes are covered as of yesterday to protect them from freezing, I still refuse, each day, to put away my patio furniture. It represents my last letting go of the sweet season just past, and against reality, I choose to refuse until the day I find myself accepting this new season and can say Yes to it. That day comes when I remember that I have lived through a lifetime of changing seasons, and that each

one holds its own gifts and leads inevitably into new weathers and wonders—some expected, and some surprisingly new.

Autumn is the most poignant season because it marks the time between abundance and apparent emptiness, between the freedom of warmth and light and the relative confinement of coldness and darkness. Unlike spring, which is also a "between season," autumn demands not only faith in the future, but trust in the process itself. Every autumn I talk myself into this trust by saying Shelley's final verse in "Ode to the West Wind": *The trumpet of a prophecy! O wind, If Winter comes, can Spring be far behind?* And so I surrender to the necessity of the season, opening myself to trust in the wondrous hidden processes of Nature, gestating new life deep down under snow through winter, and planning, under the protective cover of stark brown earth, a whole new world for spring. And I consider not only this process, but also my ability to trust it, a true Grace.

Mark Your Seasons

I resist change in my own life as stubbornly as I resist the changing of Earth into her wintertime. I am a normal creature in my resistance. There are a few gifted people who genuinely exult in the fall of the year, as I am able to do myself when I discipline my attention to focus on the beauty of the moment,

its amazing display of color in breathtaking patterns, rather than the losses implied. Acceptance of change comes not only in faith in the future, but in the ability to recognize the gifts of the present moment. And each season has its own remarkable gifts. I dare not waste them by fixating on the future to the exclusion of the unique offerings of the present time. It is a matter of balance among past, present, and future. In trust, and with the help of hidden hands, I weave these three threads meaningfully together into a beautiful pattern that is unique to my own life, and yet holds a resonance with the tapestries of all other beings as they shape their destinies.

The hidden hands that help me are angelic— and by this I mean any form that God's presence takes participating in the unfolding of the universe. Angels are merely messengers from God, and they take an infinite variety of forms. They can come in the form of other human beings, or other animals, even of trees and stones that speak to us of God's loving intention toward all beings. They can come in the form of our own thoughts, as God whispers intuitive insight and reassurance to us from within our own creative dreams and reflections. Shelley's lines are angels to me—that is, they express a truth to me and through them God helps me to accept reality and respond appropriately.

The in-between times of my life are the most uncomfortable and also the most interesting and challenging. These are the times when I know I am on my way somewhere—not where I have been, and not where I am going, but on my way. The truth is,

our whole life-span is a between season, bracketed by our birth and death which are gateways to an unknown destination. These discomfiting times throw sharp light on the reality of life as a journey, and also on the gifts we are given—the Grace—in order to make the journey well. Even the apparently stable seasons of life—the winters and summers of our souls—are not stable at all, but offer opportunity for incorporating and celebrating where we are in the time of our lives.

Way Stations

All our life seasons have rhythms. To be alive is to be in a state of constant change, however apparent or unapparent that change might be. Think of the act of breathing, or of walking. We breathe in, we breathe out, and in between there is a microsecond's pause of assimilation. The same with walking, an act which requires us to achieve balance through continuing imbalance—one foot always off the ground, yet with a steady rhythm of alternation, and again, a microsecond of rest as one foot lifts off just while the other finds its holding place. In a broader sense, we receive what we need to endure our transitions by allowing ourselves the right rhythms of our going between. We alternate between waiting and engaging, resting and working, listening and speaking. These rhythms of rest and resumption of effort are

the hallmarks of all transition. Rest is not removal
from reality, but an integral and necessary part of it.
My dictionary says that rest is a station on a journey—a stopping place where one waits for and finds
the appropriate mode of transportation and needed
maps and guidance to continue the journey. So in the
way-stations of each night's sleep, our dreams lighten
and guide us while our bodies carry on the essential
rest-work of cell renewal. Sometimes we may appear
to our friends as if we are sleep-walking through a
time of our lives, but this may not be true. We may
be engaged in important, hidden gestation, and when
the green shoots of a decision break the surface of our
lives, our friends may be in for a surprise. If their
observation was correct and we had been moving
through our days unconsciously, we will wake up
anyway sooner or later. Life requires it. We will be
called into the rhythms of renewal.

Discover Meaningful Metaphors

Whether I am between jobs, between places,
between loves, or between dreams, transition is a
time when I am uncertain about who I am, for my
self-image in relationship to my body, my work, my
place, my love, or the world is changing. It helps me
to find a metaphor that has the power of meaning to
carry me through. When I was in transition between
life in the midwest and life in western Oregon, I

wrote in my book, *At the Foot of the Mountain,*[1] about certain reassuring ways of perceiving my move through metaphor:

> It is a pregnant time for me. I am pregnant with the future in a focused way. I am pregnant with choice. I yearned for this pregnancy, yet, at times, and even now, I dread it. I do not like the loss of the familiar: my familiar body, my familiar habits. So many changes give way to make room for new life. Then there is the suffering of wait. Of weight and wait. I am heavy with something I do not yet know, have not yet named, and I grow different each day because of it. I long for it to reveal itself. I long to give it a name. Yet I do not know what it is. I must wait on the will of heaven and discern how best to respond and move with it moment by moment . . . . Now, it seems, is the time for patience and trust, and nothing more. Alas! And Thank God.

It was a wilderness time for me, between the slavery of my old, self-confining attitudes, and the promised land of new thinking and new dreams-come-true. I thought of forty years like this in the story of Moses and Miriam out of Egypt, and the forty days of Jesus between his private and public lives when he went to be alone in the wild. Transition can be a wilderness season. I wrote, "What can be learned in forty days in the wilderness! The time

and place call for deep-down change. The transfiguration of the inner self. The opening and yielding of hidden places within. Time to let seeds fall. Time to prune trees and cut away the old excesses so the whole plant can grow more freely and truly. Time to gather leftover leaves from fall. Time to open the garden. To live leanly. To put down the fat that warmed us through winter and lighten up. To move more freely. To get outside . . . ourselves. *To look at the gifts of time* —this is how to *observe* a holy season." My metaphor had taken me safely from winter to spring, and a new transition toward fulfillment. The future remained unknown, but the promise of the way being worthwhile seemed more accessible. I worked the garden of my life with a spring metaphor. Being between became easier.

Be Patient and Open

If you feel lost in a passage of your life, be patient. Get all the help that you need, and also know that you have what you need within you. Pray to be open and flexible. Prayer opens us to the Grace that is always there. Pray for patience and trust in your life. Befriending change is wise in the wilderness. Look around your life and observe where you are. Weave your times together—attentively. As I wrote to myself in my own coming home:

> Breathe. In and out. Fully. Open the inner senses. Receive and release. You are an essential part of the universe. You belong here. Receive and return the gift of life. Complete each breath. Do not put your foot down to intercept this immediate moment of Grace. Stay awhile. Attend. And I could hear the Holy One, a sweet wild voice within my trembling heart: "I am with you now, and I am waiting for you."[2]

There is an old saying in the wisdom tradition of India: "When we breathe out, God breathes in." We breathe in as God breathes out as well.

Stay on your path. Keep breathing. And go with God.

Continue Becoming the Person You Want to Be

The future is like death —
Unknown —
and requires as much faith.
So Becoming
is like Dying.

The lapse between
a single inbreath/outbreath
a slash or question
mark in time,
the act of transformation
the monarch butterfly knows.
It flies alone.
Sometimes the dead do not know
they have died.
Sometimes the winged one dreams
itself a cocoon.
Everlasting Change comes,
all the same.[3]

Prayer Reflections

On these meditation pages, you may write
your own prayers, poems, questions and insights in
response to the theme of Grace in transition. Use the
quotations on each page as a launching point for
your own reflections. Keep your notes as an intimate
part of your spiritual journal, or share them with
soulfriends and companions on your spiritual
journey.

Transition

I find myself
in the time between
selves.[4]

I watch and wait,
half-blind, keeping time
with the butterflies
in my heart.[5]

Soon, I will be full-ripe
with my Self,
able to nurse on sweet nectar,
free and light as living rain.
Soon, I will fly.[6]

We come to birth and being from God, but mystery and meaning must unfold, and what we become depends on our response to the whole of life. We create our lives as we surrender to the larger mystery that contains us. No part of our lives can be separated from any other. The journey back to the Source never leaves the Source. All is one. All is alive. We shape our souls by the choices we make and most of all by what we love. And we never stop becoming ourselves.[7]

Through sometimes impossible, impenetrable obstacles—now and then losing my way, alone and with others—my life has been a relentless quest for wholeness and authenticity in the actualization of a calling I could not deny.[8]

The Elements Are in Charge

We live in a place where
only the elements
are really
in charge,

and we are
all subject
to change,
and

the truth is,
we are in need
of comfort.[9]

Make Friends with Your Fear

$\mathcal{I}$T WAS THE FIRST TIME IN MY LIFE THAT I saw the sky turn green. It was a hideous, sick-making green, all the more ghastly as it overtook the noonday sky. I was alone in my home except for my father who was visiting, and who was ill. As I made the beds, I kept an eye on the western sky. The air had become very, very still. It was late April, and tornado season was in full sway in Minnesota. When I scanned the horizon in all directions I saw no inkling of a funnel, just an increasing and pervasive discoloration of the whole sky. When the first strong gust shook the house, I went to my father's room, grabbed his hand, and taking no time to explain, pulled him after me into the basement. As we sat huddled in the northeast corner, opposite the direction of the wind, my body shook in time with every tremble of the house, which seemed to be fighting to stay on its foundation. I was crying hard. Never before had I cried in sheer fear. It was truly a terrible experience. My whole being was in terror. The tornado angel passed over us. We were safe for that time around. Later, I reflected on how wise I was to be afraid, and how trustworthy my body's energy

was. Had the tornado come for our house, my fear had directed us to the safest possible place. The tears and trembling of my body were signs of the rush of adrenal energy that is every animal's physical response to danger. My adrenalin made me move fast, and that is what it's for. It activates the so-called fight or flight response, the two most common safety reactions in the face of physical danger. I was not afraid of my fear. On the contrary, I was grateful for it.

I did not have the casual attitude of native midwesterners toward weather. I was still in touch with my natural and protective panic responses. When I talked with friends afterwards, most of them said, "Oh, I just ignored the warning sirens and kept on watching my television program," or whatever else they might have been doing. In ignoring warning, and shutting down their own internal warning system of fear, they were in far greater danger than I was.

Fear is Physical

Fear is a gift that Nature gives her creatures to assist their survival and preserve their health and safety. Because the primary function of fear is the preservation of physical life, fear itself is physical. The whole body is overtaken by it. Shaking, sweating, crying are all physical signs that the body knows it is in danger. If we perceive that we are threatened,

we are empowered by our bodies to make appropriate choices in the interest of self-protection. If we perceive that another is threatened, our bodies respond in the same helpful way according to our degree of empathy or kinship with that other. The point of fear is to assist physically in the saving of lives. Fear, as a natural gift, is in itself good. It is the fear of fear, or the misunderstanding of fear, that is problematic, and potentially harmful or dangerous.

Fear is a Choicepost

We all naturally fear the unknown. This, too, is Nature's gift, but we must use it wisely. Moving into the unknown of any new situation means that we are not necessarily in charge. We may maintain control of ourselves, but we have no control at all beyond ourselves. The alternative to being desperately nervous about this is to trust that we will have what we need in any given moment, and that even should we be overtaken by some destructive power, life is large enough to offer new options and often to redeem old losses, one way or another. In my book about facing fear through a time of transition (*At the Foot of the Mountain*), I wrote:

> My idea about fear is that it is a natural tool for survival, intrinsic in creation. Human beings, however, having lost sight of it as a tool, have come to misuse it as a deter-

rent. Consider that fear is a Stop sign. The proper way to treat a Stop sign is to heed its suggestion and stop, then attend to the situation by looking and listening in all directions, basing the decision to move forward in the direction of choice on the information gleaned by our attention. We may move straight ahead or turn. Or we may see that we are off course, and turn around. The sign offers us the opportunity to make a free choice based on accurate information, by making use of all our discretionary senses and our ability to discern the presence or absence of danger, then decide which action and timing are most appropriate.

Sometimes making a "reality check" is difficult, and we need to match our own perceptions with those of others whose observation we value and trust. It is all right to wait at the Stop sign until you are confident enough in your choice—just don't build your house around it and refuse to move! That is the mistake many of us make. We are afraid of the Stop sign itself! We are afraid of our fear. We forget that it is there only to serve us, to tell us that this is a time or place in our lives that requires paying special

attention and taking extra care. That is all. Fear does not predict an outcome, it merely calls us to make wise choices true to the circumstances.

Name Your Fears

Fear originated in Nature for the physical protection of all creatures, but sensitive beings understand that fear is a gift for our spiritual protection as well. It serves to help us protect our total integrity, as physical, spiritual, and moral beings. If we are threatened on any of these levels, fear shows us in the same way. A symptom of our fear of fear common to human beings is holding the breath when we need it the most. Breathing hard is the natural fear reaction with the extra charge of adrenalin, but if an animal decides its safety lies in making itself invisible, it will camouflage itself and become as still as possible—seeming even to hold its breath. We humans get into trouble when we literally hold our breath! If you feel afraid, remember to keep breathing—in and out all the way. When we feel emotionally or morally threatened, we are most inclined to hold our breath—sometimes making it a chronic habit, spending a lifetime of depriving ourselves of the air we need in a complete inhalation and the release we need in a complete exhalation. Chronically frightened people don't breathe well. The first thing to do is breathe again, give the brain oxygen it needs to make a clear evaluation of the situation.

This means naming our fears. People who are chronically fearful are usually afraid of some emotional threat. This often comes from a real emotional threat experienced very early in life—perhaps through being the target of verbal and emotional abuse as a child. Really listening to one's fear can reveal the original source of it. Then the rational part of ourselves can speak to the fearful child inside, giving assurance of protection, and describing clearly how reality has changed—the old threat was real, but it is gone. The body can let go of fear, no longer in its control, but in right and respectful relationship to it as an invitation to find out what is real.

Ordinarily, I am no longer afraid of the weather. I live on the Pacific Coast now, and though we need to be realistic about the possibility of earthquakes, it doesn't dominate my daily awareness. Now I am more alert to my spiritual fears—of not always knowing how to express and give what I am called to give; of overlooking (or underlooking) life's gifts to me; of missing my destiny and wasting God's and my time; of sleepwalking through a miracle—my own life! I have the natural fear of death that motivates all creatures to stay alive, but as a moral being, I am less afraid of physical death than I am of missing life—of failing to live each moment of my life to the full. In fact, facing my inevitable death motivates me to remember how precious each moment of life is, and to respond to it with all I can give, including complete receptivity. By listening to my natural fear of mortality, I let it give me the gift of awareness and

gratitude for life. Naming the fear is the beginning of transforming our consciousness and shifting our focus from the object of fear to its alternatives.

That goes for the other things I naturally fear: being very sick and alone, suffering more loss, or losing independence and autonomy in old age. Naming these fears empowers me to examine how realistic they are, and to imagine different ways in which I might respond to these fearful situations. Always, I pray for courage to come through a peace-giving image.

Fear Can be the Threshold to Freedom

I am free to engage my mind and my emotions in conversation with my fear. It leads me to discover my own ignorance or unconsciousness. When I ask, "What do you have to show me?" it responds, "Open your eyes." I heard a story about a woman terrified of cows. One day she took a basket of apples into the small herd next to her own pasture. She intended to end the misery of her obsessive fear by letting the cows kill her! They licked her, instead, taking her apples, innocent of her true purpose. When she finally opened her eyes, she had no choice but to see and accept the gentleness of these animals. She released her fear in the strength of reality.

A phobia is an obsessive and unrealistic fear. It is usually displaced fear. I am not really afraid of spiders, or serpents, or wind—but of certain of their characteristics in myself or someone else whom I choose not to fear directly. The phobic objects are scapegoats. We can cure ourselves by learning everything we can about them. We may have a natural fear of spiders or serpents because some of them are genuinely venomous. In meeting up with one, it's good to know which are and which are not. Yet, they are also children of God with purpose and a right to be here. Serpents are ancient symbols of wisdom, eternal life (because they can form a circle), healing (their venom can be, in small doses), and even resurrection or transformation—they shed their skins and seem to be newborn. In some mythologies, spiders are respected symbols of the Great Weaver who created the universe. And my old fear of wind is softened when I remember that it is symbolic not only of the destructive and creative power of the human spirit, but of the Holy Spirit of God, as well. The more I know, the more I am free from unrealistic fear, and the more able I am to learn right responses to danger from my fears which are real in their focus.

Be Confident and Realistic

When Mt. St. Helens first threatened to erupt, I was alarmed and afraid. I had grown up just forty miles from it and never "realized" its real power as a

live volcano. I enjoyed the illusion that it was just a lovely mountain. To deal with my fear, I began to study volcanos. I learned that they are the means whereby Mother Earth sends the richest nutrients up from the core and mantle to the crust, the surface of Earth where we live. When Mt. St. Helens did erupt, my aunt in Spokane shoveled white ash around her rhododendrons, and they grew to more than double their usual size that year. I learned that, while the immediate, short-range effects of volcanic eruption are devastating, the long-range effects are immensely beneficial to the Earth. They are creativity and nurture at work. Seeing them a little more from Earth's perspective, I am much less afraid of them. Still, I am not stupid. I keep my distance from Mother Earth's construction zones.

Now I ask of my fears: Are you realistic? How can I really be harmed (or how can someone I love be harmed)? What can we do to prevent it or to help? How can I take better care? Finally, is this fear really mine, or one I inherited unconsciously from someone else? I may not have to carry many of my fears—those which are not real, and those which are not mine in the first place, but ones I have acquired out of habit. Asking the right questions clarifies all of this.

As I become more informed, I am more at peace about the purpose of the Great Design. Volcanos are wonderful. So is the wind. And creatures I learned to hate and fear I can learn to love and respect, for we are all kin in life. We each have our own beauty and purpose. We belong. Whatever

temporary harms may come as we get in each other's way, I can learn to entrust to the transforming power of God, the Great Designer who alone can see how the whole pattern holds together.

For you and for me, my prayer is that we learn each day how to live with more confidence, understanding, co-operation, and trust in the Great Design—that we learn more and more how to be.

Be

Reality is intricate and vast.
    You are real.
Life is cosmically generous.
    You are gifted, alive.
The universe holds.
    You are embraced, you belong.
It is enough.
    You are enough.

Do not be centered in
your self or the world,
but be a Self centered in God.

Love and let love.

Listen—Life is in love
with you!
Your life longs for
your trust.

Your life holds
and graciously
carries you through.

Every breath is an act
of faith and courage.

Your body believes.

Breathe.

Be inspired and let go.
Be faithful.
Be brave.

Be.[1]

Prayer Reflections

On these meditation pages, you may write
your own prayers, poems, questions and insights in
response to the theme of befriending your fear. Use
the quotations on each page as a launching point for
your own reflections. Keep your notes as an intimate
part of your spiritual journal, or share them with
soulfriends and companions on your spiritual
journey.

I see myself a cell inside an opaque prison of fear. I locate this in my body somewhere near my solar plexus, in my bowels, and encasing my throat. It is a long, narrow membrane that begins in my bowels and is cut off at the choking closure of my throat, just before the organ of utterance. The membrane is a watery blue color, like a giant seablue teardrop that fills the cavity of my body and encloses it to keep me empty.[2]

My fear seems relentless and
solid. I know it has thinness
and is not substantial, but this
doesn't matter.   I am as
locked within it as within hard
cement.[3]

I felt that I had been
stuck in the middle of a
bridge for a very long
time, unable to move
forward fearing the
possibility of nothing on
the other side, and yet
unwilling to go back.
My friend reminded me
of the obvious: one foot
in front of the other! [4]

32

Now I've come back once
again to my Mountain. Each day, all
through the day, and every night in
my dreams, I practice swimming. I
revise and revive my belief in myself and in the future, and in the
presence of God abiding and sustain-
ing me. I consecrate everything,
everything, including my old fear
and disbelief, as material for deep
transformation, and I allow trust to
re-create in me and the gift of faith to
flow through me.[5]

Praying Your Way Through Pain

"*D*O YOU KNOW WHAT SHINGLES ARE?" I asked my foreign friend in our satellite overseas conversation. After a thoughtful pause, he responded, "Do you mean, like 'Shingle Bells?'"

"Oh, I wish! No, I mean a virus, an infection of the nerves. It is a very painful and long-lasting infection related to childhood chickenpox, but in adults, the virus re-awakens and attacks the nerves. It's called 'shingles' because of the blisters that form on the skin at the nerve endings. Actually, shingles are overlapping, rough wooden sections usually on the roof of a house."

"And you have these *where* on your body?" asked my friend, now with real horror in his voice.

"On my face! Just a small patch over my right temple is visible, but the whole side of my face from my jaw to the back of my head feels like a toothache. To be precise, it feels like a bad bruise that has been burned, and then scraped, and on top of that, it itches. But I'm told that I'm lucky. It's really quite a mild case. Still, I am asking for your prayers for my healing. I shouldn't like to live with this for very long."

Leaning on the prayers of many loving and concerned friends, and learning to pray my own way through pain, I am now in the ninth week of this attack, and slowly recovering myself. I am in no danger of losing my vision, which was a terrible concern to me at first, when my right eye—and then my left, perhaps in sympathy—began to feel like an exploding golf ball. That was simply the effect of extreme neurological sensitivity in a very delicate part of the human body, with the resulting protective swelling of tissue around the nerves.

I am not a stranger to either physical or emotional pain, but each instance of suffering teaches me something, and this is no exception. I believe that one aspect of what we call redemptive suffering is the willingness to learn to live more richly, to become more truly oneself through the experience. This willingness requires an open heart and a humble mind. For these, I require the love and prayerful support of my friends.

Leaning on Love

Whenever we experience pain, whether of the body or the spirit, we are reminded of the condition of being a creature. All creatures suffer. Even my roses suffer when blighted with mildew, fungus, or a virus of their own. Even light suffers, if we acknowledge the poet's perception. Goethe, famous for his

sensitive poetry, had a sensitive eye and mind as well. He conducted a series of color experiments, after which he concluded that "color is . . . the suffering of light." Suffering is the ability of a being to be deeply affected, even altered, by the encounter with other beings, and by its own inner necessities. Hunger, for example, is an inner necessity which, unheeded, can cause pain. Hunger for affection, for music, for sunlight are as real as the body's need for food. Pain always lets me know that I hunger for love, kindness, compassion, and comfort. Whether my pain is emotional or physical, my whole being is involved and suffers my own need for healing, for touch, for a caring friend, or for solitude. Pain lets me remember that I am not alone. I need to give myself the kindness I freely give my roses, as well as other human beings, and I need to receive it from others as well. Love is the great healer. Even if the body cannot recover its full wellness, well-being is always possible at a deep level of human feeling, and love is the shaper and provider of that well-being.

When I have been unable to sleep in these weeks of pain, I lean on the love of my friends and the love of the Creator expressed to me in the natural beauty of my garden, the evening sky, the stars, and all that surrounds me. I live at the foot of Mt. Hood in western Oregon, and from my window on clear mornings, the mountain is the chief of many reminders to me that I am part of this beautiful Earth, and I can draw on its beauty for strength.

Respond

This time of pain has been a bittersweet but blessed opportunity for me to remember what I had forgotten about prayer. We say, "Pray for me," or for someone we love, or for peace, but prayer is more than asking. Prayer is being—attentive, aware, and receptive. It is being in relationship to the Source, and finding access to this Source deep within. Prayer is deep listening. It is questioning. It is seeing with brave eyes and responding with brave heart to the truth of what is revealed. Sometimes, prayer is crying, moaning, dancing, laughing—prayer is our best response to the Source of Life.

Find the Hidden Gift in Your Pain

In listening deeply to God in my pain, I rediscovered what was missing in my life at the time of my vulnerability to the attack of infection. I reflected, in giving in to the need of my body for rest, and what I saw in my reflection revealed to me that I had become too caught up with being productive to the neglect of being creative. I had been too busy to relax, too overworked to play, too driven to experience the gentle healing of re-creation that a person needs each day. No wonder my poor body had to take drastic measures to get my attention! I was off my own track, and my body's direct pain was calling

me back. I even tried to ignore it at first—I don't
have time to be sick! Finally, I had to see reality and
respond appropriately. I had to receive the gift my
pain was offering: More rest, less stress. My tears in
the night washed clean the windows of my soul. I
could see my life clearly again, and restore balance to
it. I could bless my body and give it the compassion
I gave so freely to others. I could accept myself as a
vulnerable creature, a child of Earth in need of renewal. I could give in to the little death of time out
from my normal routine of attending to the needs of
others, and prepare myself patiently and gently for
the gift of renewal. I began to pray, "Into your
hands, O God, I surrender my pain. Into your heart I
entrust and rest my body, my mind, my being." And
so my soul began to receive encouragement. I gave
my body the small act of faith it needed to begin
healing itself in earnest. Through compassion for the
pain in my temples, I accepted the call back to my
innermost temple, the sacred place of healing where
God abides deep inside my soul.

Transform Your Life

    Medicine people (traditional healers or sha-mans) in all ancient cultures believed that an illness or injury, whether to the body or the spirit, was an opportunity to make oneself better than before. It was a chance to evaluate how one lived, and to make changes for enhanced happiness, health, and integrity—the matching of outer deeds with inner values.

    To help myself do this, I have surrounded myself with images that remind me who I am and how I choose to live. I am letting go of driven work and allowing myself the re-creative pleasures of creativity and play. I remember to listen to music, to greet the day and the creatures who share the place where I live. I remember to praise them and to thank God for them—the birds, the trees, the clouds, even the rain. I remember to call on my friends, just for the pleasure of sharing a few moments of the day to-gether. I remember that love is the food and fuel of my soul, and I can draw on it and send it out every-where, wherever I am. Because all creatures suffer, we are all pilgrims in pain, but more than this, we are companions in the miracle of life, who share not only frustration and longing, but also immeasurable wonder, joy, and gratitude in being alive. To remem-ber this is to be changed deeply for the better. I forget how easily I forget! That is when life calls me back, any way it can. If I ignore the gentle reminders, life will simply become more creative and direct until I pay attention. Even if I have no regret about the way

I have been living, the events of one moment offer
me a chance to live the next moment even more in
harmony with my best intent.

Remember Your Resources

If life is offering you a similar opportunity
through pain, remember that you can move through
this pain with openness to life. Let life speak to you
and show you ways to live more deeply, more aware
of your belonging in the family of all creation, a
precious part of the Earth, a child of God. In the
intimate prayer of your heart, let the One Who Is Life
speak lovingly to you—in the soothing silence, in the
healing music of your innermost core. In your relationship with others, pray yourself well. Nurture in
yourself the attitude of mutuality: you need to give
and receive love. Keep the balance. Stay open. Call
on the help of others. Let others care for you and
remind you how to care for yourself. Always listen
to what your being needs, body and soul together,
and seek appropriate help in your healing—the touch
of a friend, a massage, physical or psychological or
spiritual therapy, a more informed intellect. Even in
pain, you can be well. Even in the little deaths of
daily life, you can move deeply into the wholeness
that is the dream and desire of God for you.[1]

Prayer Reflections

On these meditation
pages, you may write your
own prayers, poems,
questions and insights in
response to the theme of
praying through pain.
Use the quotations on each
page as a launching point
for your own reflections.
Keep your notes as an
intimate part of your
spiritual journal, or share
them with soulfriends or
companions on your
spiritual journey.

If You Could Keep Your Heart in Wonder

Our love is
the unfolding
miracle

that expands
our joy
to include
our pain.[2]

The Mountain also carries my pain . . . a companion creature, sharing time and space in a common place . . . wise in her ways. I stand under her, unable to understand my own mystery or pain, yet here in this sacred stillness I receive an inkling of the meaning of my journey. In the play of shadow and light, withdrawal and sudden emergence, as I witness her volcanic agonies, I sense that I, too, am part of a meaningful Whole.[3]

I came here hurt from demanding decisions from myself that I could not make; hurt from the weight of other people's needs; hurt from the ice of other people's fears and my own. In winter I broke through the fear barrier; later, the pain barrier. And then I began to learn again to release the hurt and heal myself anew. I held my eyes on the mandala of the Mountain and held my heart on the mantra of my prayer: "Into your hands I surrender my pain."[4]

My God-center is open . . . I am alone. I carry all ways the Origin within, and I am eternally pregnant with the Creator of Life, Who is my most intimate companion, Who sings to me from within my own marrow. I am filled with Original Grace.[5]

I have lost my place.
My body has become
a foreign country.
I no longer know
its maps or rules . . .

I want to move freely
in this country and
live here again . . .
I want to feel its welcome again.
I want to be unafraid and peaceful
and know that, after all,
I was born here . . . [6]

Three Graces of Suffering, Three Gifts of Wisdom

Compassion –
     I acknowledge myself
     to be Your needy creature, God.

Incarnation –
     I accept Your call through pain
     to embrace and embody all of my life.

Consecration –
     I offer You the new energy of this pain –
     transform it into a blessing for someone
        in greater pain.

Amen.

By suffering with faith and allowing ourselves to pass all the way through pain and death, we can always discover more life on the other side. The completion of this perennial process requires that we know the moment when to let go of our pain and are willing also to sacrifice our suffering in order truly to claim new life. [7]

Meeting Your Inner Healer

$\mathcal{A}$ FRIEND WHOM I LOVE VERY MUCH HAD gone to Jerusalem. One morning he planned to go into the Old City. As he reached the Lion's Gate, he stopped. He told me later that in the moment when he would have crossed the threshold, he suddenly heard my voice saying, "Don't go in there today." He turned around, trusting the inner voice, and went to the Mount of Olives instead. Twenty minutes later, he could hear gunfire on Temple Mount marking the outbreak of the most violent and intense expression of conflict in Jerusalem in recent memory.

Last night my friend Meredith called. She told me that she had a vivid dream in which the two of us were in a small boat riding the sea waves. She was fearful until my voice in the dream spoke reassuringly to her: "Relax. You're all right. You have what you need. Trust and let go." Just as she called me from two thousand miles away, I had finished writing a piece on trust and letting go.

In both these cases I do not think it was really my voice speaking to the intuitive, receptive minds of my friends, but rather their own best, whole selves, or perhaps God, or their guardian angels speaking to them using, in both cases, the familiar and soothing voice of someone they loved.

I also have experienced such guidance from within at crucial times—and in various forms— sometimes as simple, direct decisions that spring from an intuitive instinct, sometimes through being alert to indications from outside myself, and sometimes through dreams. A few months ago, for instance, I dreamed that my right eyetooth was breaking and I went to the dentist in a large room where people were occupied in voting booths. Yesterday, at the dentist's, while she was beginning a simple filling repair on my right eyetooth, it suddenly broke. It was election day. I went to vote right after she finished working on my tooth. While previous x-rays had not revealed the super-fine crack in that tooth, I had been extra careful about it ever since the earlier dream.

What was it that gave these instances of care and guidance? There is no way that we can know for sure, but we may call on some possibilities. As I suggested, it may have been the protective presence of the Holy Spirit using the available means of access to get our attention. In the case of my two friends, it may have been an angelic intervention, using the medium of a loving and familiar voice. Or in all three cases, it may have been a manifestation of what I call the inner healer. The inner healer is the deepest core of the self, a central part of the soul which is open to direct communion with the divine energy, and which is not bound by linear time. In other words, the inner healer is that deep part of us that remains open to God, and is in fact the divine essence within the human soul that give us life and a

sense of uniqueness and holiness. It is the part of ourselves that is most truly our Self, the seed of our potential, the core Self that is free from the ravages of time and experience, that co-ordinates our growth and inspires our choices always in the direction of healing—that is, of wholeness. The inner healer sees the image of a human soul in its radiant completion. This part of our deepest being is our truly pure essence, and it is in unbroken communion with God so long as there is a conscious or unconscious will toward wholeness.

Drawing on Inner Wisdom

In ancient Greece there were hundreds of healing temples throughout the Mediterranean. People went into these temples to make contact with the inner healer through a sacred ritual. Pilgrimage to a holy place is in itself a sign of openness and receptivity to the touch of the Divine Healer. Once in the holy place, two methods were used to bring the individual into direct contact with the healing power within. One method was called incubation—literally, going into the beehive, where the sweet honey is kept. To incubate, a person went to sleep inside the healing temple after praying for wisdom and healing in a dream. Upon waking, the person would tell the dream to a scribe who wrote it down as a record for the person to keep. These scribes were the first therapists. Perhaps today we could scientifically

measure actual physiological changes in blood pressure and brain waves in such individuals rising from healing sleep as we now do following biofeedback sessions. Often, people reported dreaming of a specific Wisdom Figure—again, what we in our cultural tradition might call an angel, or a manifestation of the Holy Spirit in a form that we could understand. This Wisdom Figure offered help and guidance. The means was effective enough to last for thousands of years as a healing practice that enhanced the well-being not only of individuals, but of society. The practice was continued in Christian churches through the medieval and Renaissance periods, and in some places down to the present day. The healing and medical uses of modern hypnosis are not far removed from ancient rites of incubation.

The other method of making contact with the healer within was called the *dromenon*—literally, the *enactment*—the same Greek word from which we derive *drama*. This particular enactment was to trace, on foot, a labyrinthine pattern carved in the stone floor of the temples of healing, and again later on in the Christian churches of Europe. The most prominent and accessible of these labyrinths is carved in the stone floor of the nave of the cathedral at Chartres, and pilgrims may still walk the path of healing there on one day of the year—the Monday after Low Sunday (the first Sunday after Easter).

The idea is that through physically moving in a spiral path, a person's innermost self is activated toward receptivity to divine inspiration and healing. When an individual reached the center of the laby-

rinth, she or he would be in a deeply altered and open state of consciousness, and by uttering the words, "I remember," would indicate that union with the divine Source had taken place. The person literally re-membered the formerly dis-membered and cut-off parts of the Self—reawakened and re-embraced the wholeness within through renewed and intentional union with God. To make oneself thus open and vulnerable to healing grace was to remember the first moment of creation, in union with the heart of God, to be a witness to the birth of the universe, and to know oneself to be an intimate, integral part of the whole design of the Creator. Such awareness was in itself healing—whole-making, and indeed, soul-making, for it brought the individual consciousness and will nearer to that image of the fully realized Self longed for for each of us by God. Such knowledge based on love is true wisdom. People who walked the *dromenon* in Greek temples or the cathedrals of Europe returned to society with a new consciousness, transformed and radiant in the knowledge of the nearness and loving care of God, dwelling intimately within all beings. These people were considered messengers from eternity, having walked the path inward to meet the Source, something we think of doing normally only through our deaths. Upon their return, they were welcomed back into their community as people who had experienced a spiritual death and rebirth, able to teach and enrich others for the greater well being and enlightenment of human culture.

All Healing is Self-healing

In ancient times there was a common respect for the inherent healing power within all creatures as their birthright. God gave all of us the built-in means of self-healing and renewal. We have more or less lost the awareness of this power, but today through holistic health movements and the prolific practice of meditation, the human family is growing newly aware of how to activate our natural inner powers of renewal. We are learning again to listen within and to trust the voices we hear inspiring our consciousness. This requires intelligent discrimination, for not all inner voices are healing and wise, nor do they all wish us well. We carry in our unconscious psyches paths of access to both creativity and chaos, and we need the complete wisdom of discernment. Therefore, we need soul-friends, whether in the form of spiritual directors, counselors, physicians, pastors, or therapists who can function for us similarly to the therapists of old—with deep respect and understanding for the natural healing processes within us. Those who help us are not our healers, putting us in a passive position of healees. They truly help us to heal ourselves, using the God-given birthright we each have within. When we lose access to that inner healing power, whether for the sake of the body or the spirit, we need help to unblock the inner pathways. That is why human beings are interdependent on one another for mutual help in healing, in accom-

plishing not only our individual wholeness, but the growth and healing that the whole human family needs to realize its collective potential for goodness and wisdom. As individual maturity is attained, we reach our shared maturity as a whole. We have a long way to go, and our mutual encouragement toward commitment is the greatest help we can give each other.

Surround Yourself with Healing Images

All creatures, not just humans, have this inner power to heal themselves. Sometimes I am most clearly called to remember how to heal myself by observing the healing power of the roses in my garden, as I witness how well their immune systems cope with fungus or mildew, given just a little help from modern chemistry and human intervention.

Inner healing is not a substitute for medical treatment—it is the organism's response to it. External treatment creates the best possible conditions for the self-healing to activate. It is no longer unusual for modern, scientifically-oriented surgeons to pray with their patients before surgery, and to continue to pray with not only the primary patient, but the whole family of friends and relatives gathered around afterwards to continue to promote the healing that happens within. Sending someone in the hospital cards and flowers is really to surround them with images that can remind them that they are part of a larger family that both suffers and is healed as they suffer and are healed. Not for nothing is the laying-on-of-hands one of the oldest sources of healing—its purpose is to open up the pathways for love to do its natural healing work. All images of beauty and harmony that have special significance to an individual can help this process, as well as the loving presence of animals and the care of other human beings. Music, colors, and images from nature all have healing power to remind the individual to open all the channels for healing and let the inner and outer forces unite toward that goal. Outer images can reinforce the healing of the attitude of the individual. They can remind us to correct our negative, despairing, frustrated thoughts and counter them as soon as we catch ourselves repeating them, by creating another way of looking at things and of describing reality to ourselves. I don't have to be annoyed or irritated during rush hour traffic, for instance. Listening to classical music in my car, I can remind

myself to shift my focus to a positive attitude: I can't change the traffic jam, but I can change my attitude and take this situation as an opportunity to enjoy my music and plan my evening, visualizing pleasures to come. I can give myself serenity instead of a head-ache!

Meet Your Healer Within

As I said, God's healing power inside us may reveal itself in the form of imagery that gets our attention. This can take a familiar or a delightfully surprising form. Calming the mind and focusing attention inside the healing temple of our bodies is the way to make contact with this inner healer. Many of us have a sense of loving, unseen presences through our lives—and we use the traditional language, sometimes, of guardian angel. I am more inclined to think in terms of angelic committees, for it seems that I sometimes need a whole healing committee to push or pull me through the morass I can create for myself, or life creates for me! Whether one or many, I call on the helpers God gives me, and make a commitment to co-operate with them and point myself in the direction of healing. Here is a meditation I sometimes use, and gladly pass on to you, as you seek God's wisdom in the sanctuary of your own being:

Breathe gently, naturally, with gratitude.
Breathe . . . relax your body . . . rest . . . and
as you do this, become aware that inside
you there is a healing spirit, the resilient
radiance of your birthright.

Breathe yourself into the image of a safe
and restful place. Take yourself to your
own power spot, your place of healing, in
your imagination. Go there now and open
yourself to the inner healer. This inner
healer is awake now, and ready to assist
you with love.

Notice where you are. Find the beauty and
the protection around you, and rest in this
place in the presence of the healer who is
with you. Find an image or a color or
sensation by which you can return to this
place of healing whenever you wish . . . .
Now stay awhile. Enjoy. Feel your deep
wellness. Rest in God. Be reborn.[1]

Prayer Reflections

On these meditation pages, you may write your own prayers, poems, questions and insights in response to the theme of the inner Self-healer. Use the quotations on each page as a launching point for your own reflections. Keep your notes as an intimate part of your spiritual journal or share them with soulfriends and companions on your spiritual journey.

God is
alive and
so are we.
To live is
to flow
with
feelings, to
participate
in the
miracle of
being, and
to move
and be
moved.[2]

All life is one:
experience and
reflection, action
and evaluation,
passion and com-
passion. All is
one. In-flow and
over-flow. God
and we together.[3]

More and more, into eternity, we become who we are.
The journey that shapes our souls
is a never-ending journey.
It is a journey of perpetual motion and power.[4]

What I learn from this
is that I am awakening.
It is again time
of the morning star,
and I return with spring
to the ancient sea nest,
place where the trees
were born.

Now I can hear the call
back to the body
of those who love me,
and yield myself
to their hands.[5]

Grandma Wisdom

She knows about pain, desperation, despair
    —no omnipotence there.
She suffers with the suffering.
Her name is Compassion.

She knows about powerlessness, defeat, oppression.
    —nothing almighty there.
By virtue of the rules of the universe
    she is limited, bound as her creatures.
She suffers with us.
She endures.

When we sit at her table
    and laugh, we call her
    Grandma Grace.

When we sit in her lap
    and weep, we call her
    Grandma Wisdom.

She knows more than we
    Who She Is
    —playful, loving,
        alive, and untamed.

She answers to any name.

Healing Addiction to Perfection

$\mathcal{D}$O YOU, LIKE ME, EVER TIE YOURSELF IN A knot trying to do something *just right*? Do you sometimes lie awake at night planning your exact moves through the duties of the next day? Do you replay a scene over and over in your mind, wishing you had done or said it differently? Do you feel remorse over a small infraction of courtesy even after you've asked for and been given forgiveness? You may be a perfection addict.[1] Don't worry. You're not alone, and it isn't hopeless.

Perfection addicts are the first cousins of action addicts, control addicts and solution/salvation addicts. We get our self-worth from what we do and how well we do, and especially from how much we do. We want to fix things. We want everything to be okay with everybody all the time. And we take responsibility for making it that way. We have, in short, the world's worst job—and it is hopeless, because it's impossible and totally unrealistic.

It isn't that we perfection addicts are idealists. We are, but that isn't our problem. Our problem is that we can't or won't tolerate anything short of our ideals. We can't stand the process. And we create our own suffering because—the process is really all there is!

Learning to Tolerate Ambiguity

Life is ambiguous. Each situation has many, not just one or even two, facets. Our hope is in learning to be good explorers and experimenters, and most of all, learning to enjoy the process of looking at life from many sides and responding to it from the complex and varied layers of ourselves. This is a beginning. And it takes practice. It is open-ended. Learning to love the process is our painless but not-easy way out of our addiction. Living, like music, is an art form. But learning to play an instrument can be fun, especially if we take our mistakes lightly and laugh at our sour notes, moving on to correct them as quickly as we can, and asking the pardon of any ears we may have offended. After a long time of awkwardness, one day we may discover that we're making music! It is a natural gift for some, an acquired skill for others. Either way, it takes practice and commitment. And perfection is not an option.

The Spirit Bead

Some Native American tribes incorporate a special spiritual value into their artwork by what they call a Spirit Bead. That is, in making a beautiful beadwork necklace or other piece of jewelry, the artist will leave a deliberate flaw—a broken bead, or

a missing bead—to show and honor the reality that only the Creator, the Great Spirit, has the right to be perfect. Not only does God alone have the right to be perfect, but clearly even God finds perfection too boring. Otherwise, the created universe would not even exist! Because process is the essence of life, once a thing is perfect, it is finished, done, ended. Dead. God must truly enjoy our process—or at least the vitality of the infinite processes of creation— because they, and we, despite folly and disaster, are allowed to continue, to keep practicing.

Learn to Love and Accept Yourself

Go easy with yourself, as God goes easy with you. Give your best, yes, but don't despair when your best is less than you'd like. Keep giving, and go lightly. *You have a perfect right to suffer your imperfections; you do not have the right to be perfect.* In fact, the essence of real self-love (not selfishness) is the ability to accept your need to be in the process of becoming your best self, and allowing that process to unfold over your whole life. That is the way God loves you, and your neighbor. That is the way you can learn to love your neighbor as yourself. In life, the process is the product.

Practice Giving and Receiving Praise

Most of us perfection/action/solution addicts are so afflicted because we never heard the magic words, "You're good—you're good enough." Most of our well-meaning parents were taught that praise raises big-headed children. On the contrary—a starved ego is a sick ego, and a sick ego harms the soul. The message, "You're good enough," is not permission to stop growing. It's encouragement to continue! It's like hearing, "You're doing fine! Keep going!" or even, "That's not quite it, but try again— keep going." We need to join together and recognize our mutual need for the encouraging kindness of praise words—and practice saying and hearing them, really meaning them and really believing and receiving them. But be patient. You're learning to accept your process, so don't feel you have to be perfectly tolerant of your imperfection! Moderate tolerance will do. Practice balance. Any performer, whether athlete or artist, will agree that growth in skill is ongoing balance between self-acceptance at any stage, and the desire to continue and become even better. If that sounds paradoxical, it is.

Appreciate Your Mistakes

They are your best teachers. Once Thomas Edison was asked how he could stand to have so many failed experiments before he finally got the light bulb to work. "I had not one failure," he said. "Each experiment that didn't work taught me something I needed to know in order to arrive at the experiment that did work." Everything that happens teaches.

That's Life

This is school, Folks.
Earth School.
And everyone, everything
is a teacher.
And everyone, everything
is a student.
That is life.

We all know a little of this,
a little of that,
a lot of some, and
none of a lot.

And every day there are
assignments: try this,
get through this,
learn from this,
pass on what you know.

And all the work is homework.
And there are gold stars.
But no one fails.
You stay where you are
until you are ready
to move on.

And everyone has the right
to ask and to learn,
to not know and to know,
to give and take,
and to grow.

Everyone needs tests
and time out,
recess and retakes,
and once in awhile
recovery leave and
incompletes.

And everyone has the opportunity
for health education and
independent studies and
special original projects
and personal, individual tutoring.

And everyone has the power
of a surprising, unique
show-and-tell offering
to the whole.

And sometimes we each feel
left out, too slow,
embarrassed, too fast,
and entirely unsure.
And sometimes it is boring.
And sometimes it is confusing.
And sometimes it is frightening.
And sometimes it is impossible.

And that is school, too.
The impossible can teach us
respect for boundaries and
limitations and the necessity
of thinking and feeling for ourselves.
The impossible gifts us with the power
to turn ourselves in new directions
and to choose.
And everything that happens teaches.

When we graduate
there is a lot of crying
and some laughter. And later,
we get to use everything we learned here
out in another real world.
And that will be school, too.
God's graduate school.

And then there will be a big Spring Dance,
and everyone will come and everyone
will have partners as needed
and they all will be pleasant and

sweet-smelling and no one's toes
will ever get stepped on, for
everyone together will be in true step
and true rhythm, including all blessed
differences and distinctions that
will still add an infinite interest.

And then we will all learn to
play and love together in a place
where everything is possible.
And that will be wonderful.
And that will be life, too.[2]

Thou Shalt Be Thyself

Many of us have been contaminated by a
distortion of the words of Jesus. In our Christian
tradition, we are victims of the perfection heresy.
Jesus is quoted as saying, "Be perfect." Rather than
"perfect" the translation should be, "Be yourself, the
person God intends and dreams for you to become.
Grow into your true self. Be really who you are
moment to moment, the best you can be in that
moment, and complete. You will never be 'perfect,'
but you can always be complete, containing all complexity, all the broken and whole parts of yourself."
To live by these words is to live a nurtured life. It is
to learn to love the way itself, and to learn to play as
well as work along the way. Jesus also said we

cannot enter heaven unless we become like children—open, trusting, honest, playful. Play is an excellent healer of the addiction to perfection and the overdrive toward doing as an end. Being is a beginning, but doing is not an end. Being is the foundation of everything else. Our doing rests on our being. It doesn't justify it. It expresses it. And so does play, the pure pleasure of expression, delight in our being.

Those of us in or touched by the Christian tradition can draw on the purity of its message and remember the core message of the love incarnate in Jesus, and gently move into our own healing with acceptance of that love in our lives.

What Jesus Really Said

Not much.

> I am
> here
> now
> with you.
> I see you,
> God-in-you.
> I need to touch you.
> I need you to touch me.
> I need to be alone.
> I will not leave you alone.
>
> Respect all beings.
> Be compassionate.
> Take risks to help others
> and to become your whole self.
>
> Be present in every moment.
> Love as fully as life allows.
> Live as fully as love allows.
> I love you.
>
> Let yourself be loved.
> Accept acceptance.
>
> Remember me.[3]

Prayer Reflections

On these meditation pages, you may write your own prayers, poems, questions and insights in response to the theme of healing a spiritually crippling perfectionism. Use the quotations on each page as a launching point for your own reflections. Keep your notes as an intimate part of your spiritual journal, or share them with soulfriends and companions on your spiritual journey.

Open your eyes to your freedom and great power to love, and the contradictions will harmonize into a single binary truth: nothing is perfect and everything is perfect![4]

The freedom to create is also the challenge to take risks, and it requires the accompanying courage to make mistakes. I have made my share of mistakes through my own process. I have learned from them, but I shall doubtless continue to make new mistakes, since they are inevitable in growth and human relations.[5]

After Dismembering

Not fixed perfection but
again-and-again completion,
unfolding, open-circling.

To re-member your Self
is to for-get
to get (Be)fore pain
to what you are
deep down.

To re-member your Self
is to for-give,
to give (Be)fore to your Self
blessing: healing from
the wound by means of the wound
itself; and
comfort: deep strength with
deep peace.

Bless you. Be comforted.
From the moment
that holds you,
begin anew.[6]

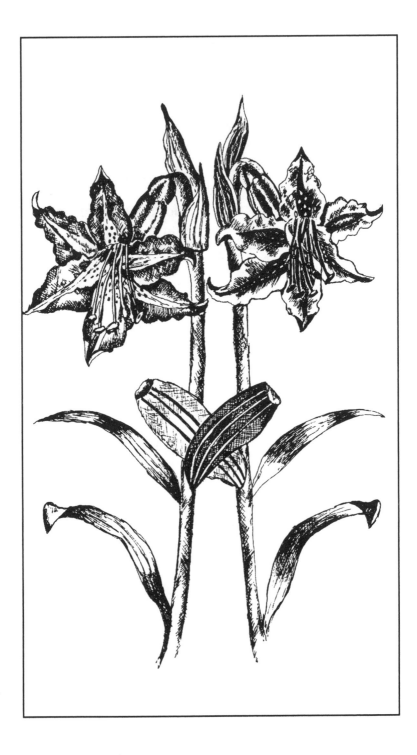

When Good People do Bad Things

$\mathcal{A}$ CERTAIN POLITICAL FIGURE RECENTLY remarked in a television interview, "I'm a good person who did bad things." During a campaign blitz, journalist Ellen Goodman was moved to ask in her weekly column, "What do you do when good people are in favor of bad things and bad people are in favor of good things, and when it's hard to tell them apart?"

Goodman had no answer.

We find ourselves living in an age of moral turbulence. On the one hand, good and evil seem set in bold relief and we think we can make clear choices. On the other hand, the moral picture keeps its drama but loses its clarity, and we are genuinely confused. How we go about our business in the voting booths reflects the dilemma: Do I vote to cut property taxes and deplete the school district's primary source of income because I feel personally overstressed by higher and higher assessments? Or do I forfeit self-interest and vote altruistically? Do I vote to shut down a nuclear power plant unless it can pass certain safety standards, or do I slide in favor of keeping it open to keep down our utility costs? I can vote in favor of mandatory recycling—unless I or my

cousin happen to be employed by the packaging industry. Over and over we are asked to choose between self-interest and the common good. How far can an individual conscience stretch?

As far as it can.

Good People Can Make Bad Choices

Good and evil are sometimes unmistakable polar opposites. More often they ride a continuum, a moral spectrum made up of a multitude of individual choices each of us makes on a daily, hourly basis. People who are basically committed to life and love and mutual respect can still fall short of their own intentions. The countless stresses of daily life work on us to distort our wills and dissolve our moral integrity. In the incidents in which we make secret, selfish choices, we are allowing our will to erode. It isn't one or two small bad choices that turn us from good people into evil people. It is the subtle ability to talk ourselves into "just one more" selfish choice—and then another—that slowly works against us to corrupt our will and make us wake up with a shattered integrity and a spirit in distress. Worse, we might not wake up, but continue unconscious of the change in our spirit, skillfully deluding ourselves into thinking the way we are is still all right because, after all, "it's just this once" that I'm cheating my own conscience. How many one times make up many?

Maybe the will never actually changes from aiming itself in the direction of conscience to choosing evil, but it can ignore conscience, which amounts to the same thing.

The present decade is marked with wonders—the end of wars and oppression, the healing of separation and the increase of commitment to healing the environment, and at the same time, increase in drug-related crimes, domestic violence, and worldwide terrorism and torture on a new scale. The extremes get more extreme. Yet there is a middle ground of despair or indifference. These times are similar to the way things were several decades ago, when Dr. Martin Luther King, Jr., was moved to speak these words:

> History will have to record that the greatest tragedy of this period of social transition was not the vitriolic words and the violent actions of the bad people, but the appalling silence and indifference of the good people. Our generation will have to repent not only for the words and acts of the children of darkness, but also for the fears and apathy of the children of light.

We live now in a time when good citizens turn their backs when hate crimes are being committed in their neighborhoods, and innocent people of color are bludgeoned to death because they happened to cross the path of a self-hating, ignorant white person, or children of color take out their rage in gangs against unarmed white women or men.

People Who Choose Evil Can Sometimes Do Good

This adds to the confusion. There are people who fight for their right to be ignorant and cruel—what psychiatrist Scott Peck calls "militant ignorance."[1] These people are basically committed to the sadistic, systematic destruction of others (and indirectly themselves) by the tyranny of their willfulness and hatefulness. Nevertheless, people thus clearly committed to evil can still sometimes inadvertently or even intentionally do good things.

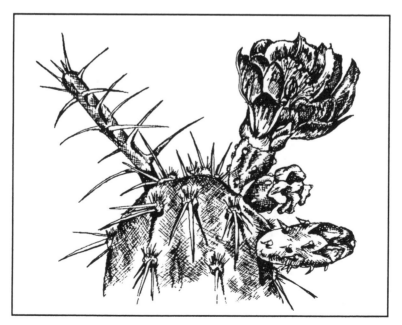

My morning newspaper recently confronted me with a strange story along these lines. It seems that for some years a contingent of the Mafia has dominated the remote mountainous region at the southeastern tip of Italy. They use natural caves there to imprison their victims. But they also are the ones who put out the forest fires. Twenty-seven thousand national forest guards patrol the vast area, but it is members of the Calabrian branch of the Mafia who, for an era, have protected Nature from human carelessness and aggression! This, incidentally, will soon stop, as the Italian government intends to oust the Mafia and turn the area into a national park.

I shake my head and meditate on this. The thought comes to me that this may be an example of God "turning all things to good," but it is beyond me.

Looking at Contradictions in Ourselves

My conclusion is a reminder to stay honest and realistic about human complexity. I, even in my commitment to life, love, and respect, am just as capable of committing atrocities as any sadist or contract murderer. I know this to be true when I feel anger rise within me, a "righteous" anger inspired by my sense of outrage against those others—the "real criminals"—who are obviously evil. I know it to be

true when I see pictures of protestors bearing signs of hate and physically attacking KKK marchers in Washington. When we respond to hatred with hate, evil wins. If I forget that I am just as vulnerable to evil as anyone else, I am in serious danger. If I remember and accept that reality, I may be able to go on resisting evil.

The poet Walt Whitman helps me to remember the fragility and strength of human nature when he says, "I am not the poet of goodness only, I do not decline to be the poet of wickedness also."[2] Yet, he was essentially a good person. He chose life and love, he lived with deepest respect for all others. He was strong enough to remain true to his values because he knew and accepted his capacity for evil.

How Goodness is Eroded

Scott Peck, whom I quoted earlier, describes human evil as the result of laziness and selfishness. Our laziness lets us take the easy path and refuse responsibility for our own actions and decisions by invoking some authority—the Church, the State, our family, tradition—whatever. In the name of obedience or group acceptance we can let ourselves do the unthinkable. This is fortified by the will to protect one's own personal ego from self-knowledge, even at the expense of the well-being of others.

We all are capable of being vulnerable to these forces, especially under stress. In his book, *People of The Lie*, Peck explains:

> If we grow out of evil and narcissism, and since we normally regress in the face of stress, can we not say that human beings are more likely to be evil in times of stress than in times of comfort? I believe so. We asked how it happened that a group of fifty or five hundred individuals—of whom only a very small minority could be expected to be evil—could have committed such a monstrous evil as MyLai. One answer is that because of the chronic stress they were under, the individuals . . . were more immature and hence more evil than would be expected in a normal situation. As a result of stress the normal distribution of goodness and evil had shifted in the direction of evil . . . . Having considered the relationship between evil and stress, it is appropriate to comment on the relationship between goodness and stress. [A person] who behaves nobly in easy times—a fair-weather friend, so to speak—may not be so noble when the chips are down. Stress is the test for goodness. The truly good are they who in time of stress do not desert their integrity, their maturity, their sensitivity. Nobility might be defined as the capacity not to

regress in response to degradation, not to become blunted in the face of pain, to tolerate the agonizing and remain intact.[3]

How Evil is Counteracted

Dr. Peck suggests that we can only counter evil in ourselves. The point is, if enough of us do that, evil will be overcome and humanity can be healed. It isn't by "doing good" that we counter evil. It is by loving. If evil is primarily the energy of hatred and the will to destroy, then the opposite of evil isn't mere goodness—which can be passive or sterile—but the intention and the commitment to love—to think and act lovingly toward others and oneself for the sake of enhancing the well-being of all and the quality of life.[4] Love is the basic recognition that we are all part of one body—we are literally parts of the body of Earth, inseparable from her and from each other, and also part of the Source of all creation, God. We are what Christian theologians call the Body of Christ. Evil is the attempt to separate, to destroy the integrity of humankind, of Earth, of creation, of the individual soul, and of all union with God. Love simply unites and creates more love. Love doesn't love evil, but it loves the victims of evil—including those who choose and perpetrate it. Love can pray for healing for those who are wounded in their souls by their own attempt

to cut themselves off from the whole body that contains us—the creative body of cosmos held in the heart of a loving God.

And, in love, I can pray for my own continuing healing, for my acts often separate me against my overall will, and I am in daily need of forgiveness and reconciliation. I daily resist the harm of soul-murder—the demoralization of others—and also of spiritual suicide—the defeat of my own psyche. As I genuinely open myself to forgiveness, I can freely offer it to others who genuinely desire and ask for it. We are ready to be forgiven only when we can redirect our will and return to harmony with our desire for the well-being of all beings. To ask for forgiveness with no intention of change is to lie. Being forgiven means being empowered by love to change our lives, to make amends and to be healed.

Finally I think there is healing and reconciliation in remembering the Beatitudes, especially, "Blessed are the merciful for they shall obtain mercy." We need mercy toward ourselves, but a searing mercy, not a sentimental one. Real mercy is the passionate, loving belief that we can always make new choices for the common good, transcend our fears and insecurities, and come home to our best selves, to God, and to each other's best selves, learning together to forgive, to grow, and to become whole.

Godspeed and be merciful to us all.

Prayer Reflections

On the following meditation page, you may
write your own prayers, poems, questions and insights in response to the theme of human complexity,
and our universal propensity for evil in particular—
beginning with the power of each individual to make
choices from ill-will or good will. Use the quotation
as a launching point for your own reflections. Keep
your notes as an intimate part of your spiritual journal, or share them with soulfriends and companions
on your spiritual journey.

Do I contradict myself?
Very well then I contradict myself,
(I am large, I contain multitudes.)
                        Walt Whitman[5]

When Love Means Letting Go

$\mathcal{W}$HEN I WAS A CHILD MY GRANDMA WAS my best friend. We read and laughed and cried together. She taught me to love poetry and Pogo and Shakespeare and mangos. Her four children adored her. I was privileged to be her closest grandchild—both in proximity and spirit.

When I was seventeen, Grandma experienced a medical crisis, a disease progression that resulted in her needing a double amputation. Her physicians told us frankly that they did not expect her to survive the surgery, but that without it, her dying process would be long and excruciating. In preparation for this drastic procedure, my aunt and I went to the hospital chapel to pray for strength and guidance for all of us—especially to pray for the grace to help the woman we both loved so deeply. My aunt was angry. She was not ready to face the prospect of letting go of her mother, and she was furious at God for forcing it on her. I was simply heartbroken—that my favorite person in the world was suffering, and might suffer even more, regardless of any decision we all would make in her behalf.

In the end, we all agreed to the inevitable conclusion of the medical recommendation. None of us wanted Grandma to experience an agonizing

death. Then the conflict began. During her operation, I prayed that Grandma could die peacefully. Her children prayed that she would survive. My prayer was out of one kind of love, and their's was out of another. Grandma had often said to me in our intimate times together that the one thing she truly

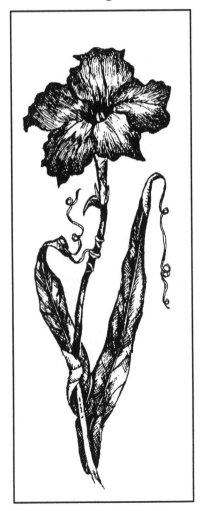

dreaded was the possibility that her body would outlive her mind, or that she would become so physically incapacitated that she would spend years of her life helplessly and completely dependent on others. My Grandma had raised her children alone during the Depression, and worked hard through World War II to keep them together, and both her shipyards job and her boarding house demanded all the strength she had. Her dignity had always sprung from her strength and sense of personal independence and competence. Her doctors had told us that if she survived this surgery, she would not only wake up

without legs, but possibly without her rational personality or faculty. I could not bear that idea. I had come to understand exactly how important her intellect was to her, and how much she valued her physical autonomy and freedom. Her children, who had more years of experience and more complexity in their relationships with their mother than I had, were primarily focused on their need to continue their relationship with her—to rely on her powerful spirit as they always had, and to finish whatever may have been unfinished between them. Also, they were simply not as close to her in those latter years as I had become, and they had not heard her express her specific fears as I had. All of us loved her immensely, but the focus of our love was different. As a grandchild, my relationship with this woman was not complicated as parent-child relationships always are. I could move into her point of view, and though it was not easy, I could imagine letting her go as an alternative to witnessing the living death to which she might otherwise be condemned. If it came to that, her children could make the same choice—but their first battle was with their own need to keep their mother alive.

While all this was going on in the family, Grandma meanwhile had to come to terms with losing either her legs or her life. I do not know if the possibility of losing her mind was presented to her by her physicians. No one in her family talked to her about that. For my part, when we were alone together, Grandma and I cried and kissed and said Goodbye. We talked about her anticipation and

happiness at the prospect of being with her own parents again in heaven, and with all the lost loves and friends of her life who had gone before her. And she promised to save me a spot and keep it warm for the next seventy or so of my years—which she would continue to watch over from her advantaged viewpoint in Paradise. She wanted to go, and she was ready.

But she stayed. Grandma survived the surgery and did in fact lose both her legs and her mind. Our Goodbye before her surgery was really our Goodbye, though her body lived on for another seven years. She was never again fully in it. From time to time she would have her lucid moments, and those were the worst. In them she realized what had happened to her, and she wept. Then she would drift back into merciful confusion. Her children and I still loved her and included her in our normal lives as much as we could. My father had the hardest time accepting her mental deterioration. He was impatient and angry and wanted her to be her brilliant self. He wanted his Mama back. Every time he left her, he cried. Gradually, he let go of his need for her old self and grew more patient and tender toward her new self. His sister and brothers finally came to accept not only her condition but her need to leave. Then, when they had grown accepting of it, she died. If her soul had made a choice to let her body live until her children were ready to be separated from her, hers was indeed the greatest love of all. I have always thought that she and God worked something out when she was on the operating table. Years

before she'd told me that she had almost died as a young woman but she told God that her children needed her and God had listened. Maybe God listened twice. That great love had cost her the highest price, but it would have been like her to agree to the sacrifice. She had always incarnated love to the rest of us. In all of our efforts to let go and accept what was best for each other, we went right on learning from her what love could mean. In spite of my sadness for her those last seven years, in some way, I understood. Grandma could let go of her legs—and even her wonderful mind—until her beloved children were ready to let go of her.

Grandma continued to teach me about life. Through her example I first came to understand the mystery of physical suffering and why it is so often part of the end of our lives. For those of us, like Grandma, who love this life so much, we simply could not bear to leave, would not agree to graduating from it into the Larger Life, unless it finally became too painful to continue. The body suffers, then, in the service of fostering in the soul the willingness to let go and move on.

Other Kinds of Letting Go

All grievous loss calls for our letting go. Grievous loss is that which makes us feel we have lost a part of ourselves. It is physical, such grief. It

brings physical chaos, emotional confusion, and a dilemma of the spirit if we do not know ourselves separately from the one we have lost or from what we have lost. Gradually healing comes as we re-shape our self-image and experience ourselves in new terms, and so make peace with reality. Then we are called not only to let go of what we have lost, but even to let go of the pain of that loss, which is our main link to what we have loved, during the grieving process. Sometimes we become as attached to our grief as we were to the one taken from us. Freedom comes in finding a new spiritual connection to the past and the loves of the past, incorporating that love into our present lives, making the future possible again, and the promise of fulfillment real.

It isn't only the physical death of someone we love that evokes the necessity of letting go as an act of love. Many circumstances give the same demand-ing call to challenge and refine our spirits' capacity for pure love. The outgrowing or leaving of any relationship by one partner—whether in a marriage, a friendship, a love relationship, or any other kind of partnership—makes the same demand on the human spirit to grieve and grow through the acceptance of loss as the new reality, the new condition in which life goes on. Other natural changes can evoke the same feelings—a grown child leaving the family nest; being called to a new job, spiritual community, or neighborhood; making a new home, creating a new family. Even fulfilling a dream implies letting go of the past, and we may be surprised at the discovery of our attachment to what we thought had limited us.

Sometimes it is our dreams that we need to let go, or our cherished opinions and assumptions about what is real, or right. When life takes over, we can sometimes feel small and overtaken. We are called, in those times, to grow, to expand our consciousness and our hearts to meet changing reality, to leave behind our old ways in order to live more fully, to love more deeply.

Letting Go Can Mean a Positive No

We may also be called by life to face the limitations of loss that the body knows. We grow older and the body refuses to be driven mercilessly as it was in youth. We are called to mercy, to loving the body we live in with mercy. We need to let go of the harmful habits of the past and learn to say a positive No to the temptation to overdo, to overextend our energy resources, or to undertake activity that can overstress and injure the integrity of our bodies, or our spirits. A positive No to all the too-muchness in our lives has the power to renew and revive what is most precious to us. It means a letting go of our old self-image of Godlike unlimited ability or energy, and a letting go of the demands of others as well as ourselves when those demands become harmful. Surrender to reality is saying Yes to what is possible within the limits of who we are.

Tender Loving Detachment

Loving our bodies and loving ourselves and knowing that we are worthy of that love *just because we are* give us the power to change our lives for the better. This means recognizing the attachments that will harm or kill us if pursued, and cultivating a tender, loving detachment that frees us from drivenness, dependency, and desperation. We need to be treated this way ourselves. Clinging kills. When Mary Magdalene found Jesus in the garden on Easter morning, he said to her, "Don't cling to me." He said it out of love for her and himself. He might have said, "I have things to do and so do you, to become our best selves. Let me go to fulfill my destiny, and you go also, to become your best, truest self. Discover your gifts and use them. Don't distract yourself and delay your true joy by clinging to me in this moment. I love you! Go."

My favorite of all the love poems I have written has these lines in it: "I'll be your friend, won't clench or close you;/ hold you close with open arms,/ I'll love you."[1] That's my recipe for TLD—Tender Loving Detachment. It takes a delicate balance and a lifetime of practice. It's worth it.

Love Mantra for Letting Go

I learned along the way that I have a choice when faced with a grievous loss, or the challenge to let go. I can choose to be greedy or grateful. Greed says, "This is good! I want more!" Gratitude says, "This is good! Thank you!" Greed always implies, "It isn't enough." Gratitude says "I am complete in this moment. It is enough." Greed kills. Gratitude heals. When I see that I need once again to let go, I pray my special Love Mantra for Letting Go.[2] It works like this:

Visualize what you need to let go. Bathe the image in gold light, and pour your gratitude and love into that image. If you need to let go of a person, bathe the person in love and in the gold light of God. If you are ready to let go of some negative part of your life, image it and frame it with the gold light of God. Now, say these words out loud and send them into the image:

I bless you,
I release you.

I set you free,
I set me free.

I let you be,
I let me be.

Allow the image to dissolve and be ab-
sorbed by the gold light. Rest a moment in
the presence of that light. Now wrap yourself in a soothing pink light, flecked with
gold. This is God's love pouring over you
and filling you. Receive. Be at peace . . .
Return to yourself, renewed.

Prayer Reflections

On these meditation pages, you may write
your own prayers, poems, questions and insights in
response to the theme of letting go in the name of
love. Use the quotations on each page as a launching
point for your own reflections. Keep your notes as
an intimate part of your spiritual journal, or share
them with soulfriends and companions on your
spiritual journey.

I bear down hard
on all these deaths.
Each one is unique, it's true.
As no love is the same,
no loss is.

I have to let each one
out of me separately,
give each loss the scream
that belongs to its own
love's ecstasy.[3]

I am dried out
from loss of tears.
And sometimes
there are screams.

I grow suddenly dizzy,
caught in the white-out
of an inner tundra storm.
Without focus I cannot tell
If I am going somewhere
or holding still.[4]

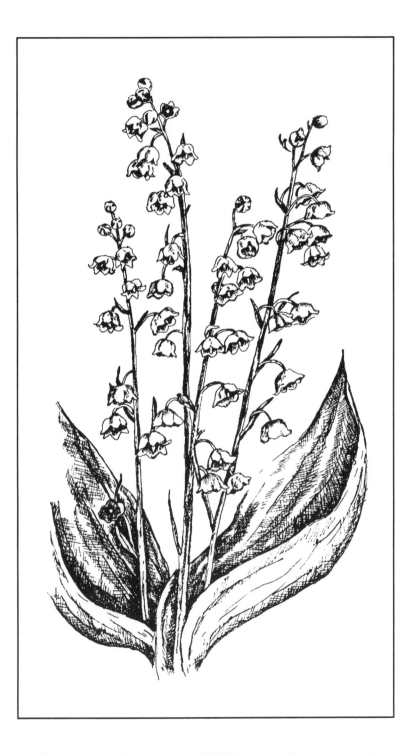

Meeting Death Can Mean Living More Deeply

Dance for Me When I Die

A woman ran through a tunnel toward the ocean
and she danced, she danced in the ocean.
A woman ran through a tunnel toward her death
and they danced, they danced for her death.

> Nobody's grandmother
> I'll be a fairy
> godmother if you
> choose me
>
> How I'd love to be
> around with roses
> when you ring forth
> in glory
>
> So make a promise
> wish for wish —
> I'll sing to all
> your rainbow living
>
> If you will laugh
> once, weep a little,
> a dance for me
> when I die.[1]

J WROTE THIS AFTER SEEING THE BEAUTIFUL FILM, "Tell Me a Riddle," from a novella by Tillie Olson. My friend Glo was dying. I had just been to see her and say Goodbye, blessing her for her journey and being blessed by her for mine. The woman in the film showed me how it was with my friend—how it would be for me in my time of what we call death, what the old Russian mystics called the transfiguration of the soul—going back into God.

Going Back into God

Earth is our mother but she is also our sister, for we both come from God. The One who in the beginning before time gave birth to the universe, shaping the cosmos in love, weaving a dream into form, extending divine energy into material essence—this is the One called by myriad names in all cultures, known by yet other names to other species and worlds, yet remaining—the One. The Source. The core of all-that-is. This One draws us individually out of the divine heart, and from the womb of eternity allows us to be born into a single, miraculous body, and entrusts us with shaping our destiny and becoming uniquely ourselves. We are not abandoned by eternity into time. Rather, we are held. The time and times of our lives are contained in the largeness

of eternity. And from time to time, we have inklings of this, all through the moments of our lives. When we are born into our bodies, and when we are born out of them back into eternity through what we call death, we are participating in the divine dance of the universe.

Born from the Womb of Time

Weeks before my young husband's sudden death, he came to hear me speak to a large group of professional healers, care-givers, and death-midwives at a convention on terminal care and death. I began with the poem I shared with you just now, and named my talk "Dance for Me When I Die—Death as a Relational Rite of Passage." Just as all of our existing relationships are changed when a new birth enters our lives, the mystery of physical death also changes the shape and texture of our bonds. It does not end them. It transforms them across the thin barriers between the time-space dimension and that of eternity. I said that we mortal beings are like fetuses held in the womb of time. Just as the growing embryo in a woman's body is part of her world, moving unknowingly through the rooms of a house, carried along on car and airplane trips, present at board meetings, movies, parties, and on trips to the dentist—so we are carried within a dimension that is real but which we cannot perceive because of the opaque, protective membrane around us that is time.

We cannot even imagine there is a larger reality beyond what we can experience in our small, wonderful world, any more than a fetus could imagine applesauce, airplanes, or the shape of its parents' hands. Yet, now and then, there may be inklings—as when a pregnant mother strokes her belly and the life inside is soothed, or the father presses a kiss against his beloved's skin and croons to the child within. Inklings. At the moment of our physical deaths, our ripened souls move forth into an unknown but expectant world. I imagine that the loving presences of those we have known who have gone before us will be there with outstretched hands to welcome us. All along, they have kept watch over us, as a family eagerly awaiting the birth of a child.

Even to speak of it this vaguely requires metaphors—the best we can do is to say, "maybe it's like this . . . or, it's as if . . . "

Neither my husband nor I could know that these words and images of my presentation were our own preparation for his birthday into Paradise three weeks later. Because our spiritual bond was so deep, and our love for each other so complete, our souls' communion was not broken by his physical death. It has changed, but it is a larger, fuller version of what it had been before. The main difference is that never again will we share the same physical dimension, and for that the part of my soul connected to my own body will grieve and suffer in missing my beloved until my own moment of transfiguration comes, bringing our reunion. But with my spirit, the part of me that is eternal, connected all along with eternity, the depth dimension of my own being—that part of me remains united with that part of everyone I love, no matter what. Even now across distances of time and space I sometimes sense the state of friends' lives, at a deep level of feeling and compassion. These qualities, I believe, we get to keep forever.

Within an hour of my husband's physical death, I could feel his wonder and joy at his new reality. It was *as if* he were a small child looking up at the star on top of a Christmas tree for the first time, and sparkling with delight from head to toe. I wanted to say, "Tell me all about it!" But I got the impression from his spirit that I had been right—we mortals have no frame of reference. I wanted details, but all I got was a remarkable assurance: It's *as if* all

the best of what we need and what we can bear is happening, and yet, *there's always more to come.* How wonderful. Infinite, eternal growth. My husband would have said, "Cosmic Wow!"

Intimacy with the Universe

After I told one of my closest friends about my husband's sudden leaving of his body—and mine—she cried to her own husband, "What is *happening* in the universe?"

"People are dying," he said.

"*Why?*"

"In order to become more intimate with the universe."[2]

I am becoming more intimate with the universe, too, because of being shattered and opened wide by the meaning I derived from my beloved's death. When my heart was broken, it was broken open and stretched so thin that it became transparent and large enough to hold an even greater love— to hold even the infinite, which holds me as well. I feel that I, too, have broken through into a larger dimension than I knew before—the time-womb around me has also stretched and grown thinner. I sense shadows of light on the other side. I feel both a more real kinship with those presences, and a deeper tenderness for all mortal beings with whom I still share the wonders and blessings of the material universe.

Also, I know my own mortality in a new way.
Even the longest human lifespan is like a wink in
time compared to the lifespan of, say, a river (the
Columbia is two billion years old!), a giant redwood
tree nearing its two-thousandth birthday, or a star
here from the beginning. My moment in time, in this
precious, fragile flesh where I live most intimately, is
the most gracious gift a soul could receive. I must
honor it. Accept it. Cherish and enjoy it. Learn all I
can from it. Most of all, I must fulfill my own time
here. I must become, under the conditions of my
birth, the person my Creator dreams and longs for
me to be, to give both of us joy. And to fulfill my
purpose among my own kind—for we are all called
to help each other in our becoming, to inspire each
other in the realization of our full spiritual growth
within the limitations of time and space. Never again
in just this way will I be given the opportunity to
focus my energy and attention on this face of reality.
Just because I am limited by my skin and senses, I am
given the chance to focus sharply on what immedi-
ately presents itself, and know it through all my
senses, including my sixth sense of intuition and my
seventh sense of wonder. And this richness, this
spiritual texture, is given to me through my mortality—because I will die, because my body will return
to Earth as my soul returns to Eternity, each moment
is of infinite value. I choose to live it as deeply, fully,
richly as I can. I choose to continue to expand my
spirit and respond fully to all that life presents, so
that, like my husband's, my life can naturally over-
flow from the fullness of its time into the fullness of

eternity. I will have a natural birth into the infinite heart of God—what the old ones call a holy death. I will burst forth from my body like a butterfly from its cocoon, a sacred place without which it could never have grown those unimaginable wings! The meaning of my own death, taught to me as I live through the deaths of those I love, is this: I am gracefully called to "live as fully as love allows," and to "love as fully as life allows."[3]

I need no skull on my desk to remind me of death and the obvious gift of life, as the monks of the middle ages did. I see my own mortal bones beneath my thinning skin; and knowing that this body will die, I bless and thank it each day for its miraculous life, for giving me the opportunity to fulfill my heart's desire for life and love.

I know, too, that from the moment of birth if not before, our bodies begin to die. Each month we grow a whole new skin! Our dead cells are constantly sloughing off and going into the food chain to be cleaned up as nutrients by the microscopic animals who live co-operatively with us. The moment when my soul leaves this body will be dramatic, but it will also be consistent with the physical process of ongoing death and rebirth enacted since my birth. We are in a constant flow of life, death, and more life. Death is not the opposite of life, but an essential part of it. Without dying, there is no living. Knowing this gives me comfort and makes that big moment of my physical death seem less strange.

Because it Means Separation

An egg
breaks,
no bird
flies, but
conception
and birth
are one:
yolk and white
separate,
at once become
two.
You cannot make them
go back to being
one.

That is death.
Do you see?
Soul and body,
separated,
on separate
journeys.

The mother of death
yesterday ate
holy communion food
with me, breaking open
seeds of the sun.

I prayed,
having fallen
into the abyss
of grief,
wanting to understand
why I am so relentlessly
hurt by death.

There came an angel
in the abyss
who took the form
of a bird.
This was its answer.

Then it offered me
a golden egg to eat,
eagle wings beating
over its essence
into a new form,
frothed together over fire,
reunited under a different
order, not to feed itself
but to feed me,
that I might live.

Separation is what makes physical death so
painful, and grief so physical. It is a separation so
complete as far as our senses go that we feel it as the
gravest possible assault to our humanity. But the
separation is temporary. When, after a lifetime of
faithfulness, I fulfill my own destiny, I will be ready

and worthy to join my spiritual ancestors. In the meantime, every separation will be softened if every relationship I'm in is complete from moment to moment—if I give my fullest commitment to the growth of each member of the relationship, and keep current by saying, acting, and living my own truth in the most loving way possible.

I pray for you as for myself the continuing healing of fear by love, and the fullness of love in a life that is truly enthused. To be enthused means to be filled with God—not only after the end of this life and the beginning of the next, but all along the way, right here, right now, and always.

***In the End When Life Begins Again and there is Only
All and Now***

After great loss
I disinhabit
my body,
disappear
into no-where
(not now-here),
become lost
in my loss.

Later,
reincarnate,
I find myself
inhabiting life,
no longer having
to imagine the past,
I foremember
the future
time-out-from-time,
when every glory ever
lived is gained again,
every precious moment
is expansive to unending,
and in the Eternal Moment
all we have to lose is loss.

Prayer Reflections

On these meditation pages, you may write
your own prayers, poems, questions and insights in
response to the theme of mortality and eternal life.
Use the quotations on each page as a launching point
for your own reflections. Keep your notes as an
intimate part of your spiritual journal, or share them
with soulfriends and companions on your spiritual
journey.

Journey

One way or another
more naked when we die
than at birth.
Emptied.

Unharnessed.
Unencumbered.
Untangled.
Allowed

for the journey
only as much
as will fit
into the hand
of God.[4]

Crosses

intersecting
upon Fire.

There are many dyings
but one Death

and many births
but one Resurrection.[5]

... To befriend the body
and its pain is to move
beyond death toward
original joy.

Remember your own
and the other's
Mystery.[6]

You belong to the land
and sky of your first cry,
you belong to infinity.[7]

You can never force your own resurrection by getting ahead of your process. All you can do is be faithful to your own death, when that is what's facing you. Because you have the courage to meet and go through your death, your resurrection will come, as spring follows winter.[8]

Why so soon?
Not soon at all —
your time is complete . . .
Nothing ever ends.
Everything is always
          beginning.[9]

The way to rebirth is in facing one's death. Labor is difficult. The labor of birth hurts . . . Yet if one can survive the pain and the work, life follows to the full. Life will be faithful to those who have faithfully worked in the service of life. The labor to die is often the same as the labor to be born. The large life inside can no longer be contained . . . How hard to open, as well as to leave, the closed garden of the past, or of the body, in either birth or death. Delivery is accomplished only in the opening.[10]

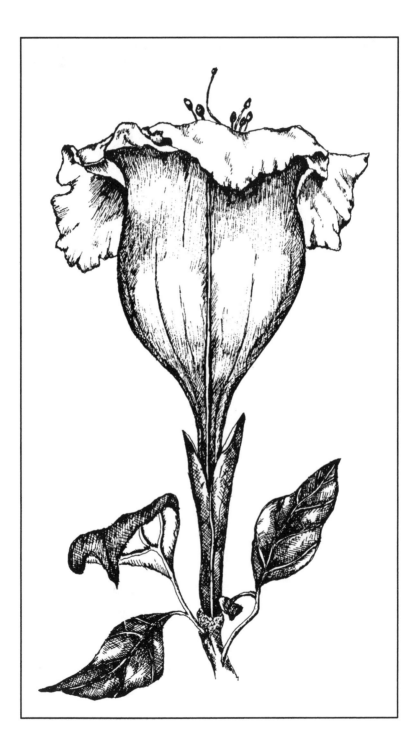

Sister Grace

—Jesus' Older Sister

She is born, first daughter,
    from Wisdom's womb.
She is fed by the breast
    over the hospitable heart of God.
She is given freely to us
    by the hand of the gregarious God.
She befriends all beings.
She is born anew in our souls
    when we openly name her,
    Guardian and Guide
    of all our lives.

May her delight fall upon you.
May her tears refresh you.
May her living colors
    flow through you
    and comfort you.
In all ways,
    may she love you
    and bless you.

Notes

CHAPTER ONE

1. *At the Foot of the Mountain: Discovering Images for Emotional Healing*, Alla Renée Bozarth, CompCare Publishers, 1990.
2. From "Passover Remembered," *Womanpriest: A Personal Odyssey*, Alla Renée Bozarth, revised edition, LuraMedia, 1988.
3. *Life is Goodbye/Life is Hello: Grieving Well through All Kinds of Loss*, Alla Renée Bozarth, revised edition, CompCare Publishers, 1986; and *A Journey through Grief*, Alla Renée Bozarth, CompCare Publishers, 1990, both distributed by Hazelden.
4. *Life is Goodbye/Life is Hello.*
5. From "Aurora Dance," *Life is Goodbye/Life is Hello.*
6. From "Chrysalis," *Stars in Your Bones: Emerging Signposts on Our Spiritual Journeys*, Alla Bozarth, Julia Barkley and Terri Hawthorne, North Star Press of St. Cloud, 1990.
7. *Womanpriest.*
8. Ibid.
9. *Stars in Your Bones.*

CHAPTER TWO

1. From the audiotape, *Reading Out Loud to God*, Alla Renée Bozarth, Wisdom House, 1990.
2. *Love's Prism: Reflections from the Heart of a Woman*, Alla Renée Bozarth, Sheed & Ward, 1987.

3. Ibid.
4. *At the Foot of the Mountain.*
5. Ibid.

CHAPTER THREE

1. A version of this meditation was published by CareNotes, Abbey Press, 1991, St. Meinrad, Indiana, and is used here with the gracious permission of the publisher.
2. *Life is Goodbye/Life is Hello* and *A Journey through Grief.*
3. *At the Foot of the Mountain.*
4. Ibid.
5. *Love's Prism.*
6. From "Loving the Body," *Life is Goodbye/Life is Hello* and *Stars in Your Bones.*
7. *Womanpriest.*

CHAPTER FOUR

1. This meditation is adapted from the audiotape and book, *A Journey through Grief*, CompCare Publishers (audiotape) 1989, distributed by Wisdom House, and (book) 1990.
2. *Womanpriest.*
3. Ibid.
4. Ibid.
5. From "Awakening," *Life is Goodbye/Life is Hello.*

CHAPTER FIVE

1. The phrase, "addiction to perfection," is borrowed from the fine work of Marion Woodman in her book, *Addiction to Perfection*, Inner City Books, Toronto, 1982.

2. From the audiotape, *Reading Out Loud to God.*

3. Ibid., and *Wisdom and Wonderment: 31 Feasts to Nourish Your Soul*, Alla Reneé Bozarth, CompCare Publishers, 1993, distributed by Sheed & Ward.

4. *Love's Prism.*

5. *Womanpriest.*

6. *Life is Goodbye/Life is Hello* and *A Journey through Grief.*

CHAPTER SIX

1. See *The Road Less Travelled*, M. Scott Peck, Simon and Schuster, 1978.

2. See *Leaves of Grass*, Walt Whitman, New York University Press, 1980.

3. *People of the Lie: The Hope for Healing Human Evil*, copyright 1983 by M. Scott Peck, M.D. Reprinted by permission of Simon & Schuster, Inc.

4. For further insight into the problem of human evil, see *Good and Evil*, Martin Buber, Scribner, 1953, *The Night and Nothing*, Gale D. Webbe, Seabury Press, 1964, and *Christian Reflections* by C.S. Lewis, W.B. Eerdman, 1967.

5. From "Song of Myself," *Leaves of Grass.*

CHAPTER SEVEN

1. From a poem titled "Loving in the Open" on the audiotape, *Water Women,* Alla Renée Bozarth, Wisdom House, 1990, and titled "Starchildren" in *Love's Prism.*
2. In *Life is Goodbye/Life is Hello, A Journey through Grief* (book and audiotape), *Love's Prism,* and *Wisdom and Wonderment.*
3. From "Reincarnation," *Life is Goodbye/Life Is Hello.*
4. From "Loving the Body," ibid.

CHAPTER EIGHT

1. *Life is Goodbye/Life is Hello* and the audiotape, *Dance for Me When I Die: Death as a Rite of Passage,* Alla Renée Bozarth, CompCare, 1989, distributed by Wisdom House.
2. See "Christmas Resurrection" in *Womanpriest.*
3. From "What Jesus Really Said," *Reading Out Loud to God* and *Wisdom and Wonderment.*
4. *Life is Goodbye/Life is Hello* and *A Journey through Grief.*
5. *Stars in Your Bones.*
6. From "All Kinds of Risings," *Stars in Your Bones.*
7. From "Belonging," ibid.
8. *Womanpriest.*
9. From "Biodance," *Stars in Your Bones.*
10. *At the Foot of the Mountain.*

Also from Sheed & Ward

Love's Prism
Reflections from the Heart of a Woman

Love's Prism sheds light on the
meaning and mutuality of love.
Love is the essential task of
human beings, and the most
difficult, confusing, and ambiva-
lent. This is a book that will
bring hope, spiritual growth, and
the fulfillment that comes from a
freshly awakened sense of the
miracle of love in our lives.

LL1044, 76 pages, paper, $4.95

Wisdom and Wonderment
Thirty-one Feasts to Nourish Your Soul

"This book, written in crystal-
clear, poetic prose, provides
practical advice for approaching
life more meaningfully. It offers
life-giving food for the hungry
spirit and life-sustaining drink for
the parched soul." — Rolf
Gompertz, former Director of
Media Relations, NBC

LL1803, 102 pages, paper, $9.95

To order, write: Sheed & Ward
                        P.O. Box 419492
                        Kansas City, MO 64141

Or call: 1-800-333-7373